Up-a-do Unlimited Presents

Popular 8 Note Songs for Christmas

Patterns for Xylophone, Glockenspiel, Recorder, Bells and Piano

By Debra Newby

This book is for beginning musicians, parents, grandparents, teachers and all others who support and encourage the arts and music, with special thanks to the Up-a-do Unlimited Crew — family and friends who also believe that every individual has unlimited potential.

Copyright 2017 by Up and Over Educational Services. All Rights Reserved. No part of this book may be reproduced, scanned, or distributed in any printed or electronic form without permission. Upado Unlimited, 9800 El Camino Real #188 Atascadero, California, 93422

ISBN – 13:978 – 1548256241

www.UpadoUnlimited.com

Contents:

Greetings	4	5. While Shepherds Watched	16
Many Instruments to Play	5	6. Up on the Housetop	17
Beat, Rhythm and Tone	6	7. Deck the Halls	18
Music Notes and Rhythms	8	8. Angels We Have Heard	19
Artistry	9	9. Joy to the World Melody	20
Taking it Step by Step	10	10. Joy to the World Harmony	21

Songs with 4/4 Rhythm:

11. Boyce Hallelujah - A Round   22
12. Mozart Alleluia - A Round   23

1. Jingle Bells   12
2. Jolly Old St. Nicholas   13

Songs with 3/4 Rhythm:

3. Good King Wencesles   14
4. Go Tell It on the Mount.   15

13. Christ Was Born   24
14. I Saw Three Ships   25

Contents:

Songs with 3/4 Rhythm:

15. Over the River	26	
16. Midnight Clear	28	
17. Come A-Wassailing	30	
18. Bring the Torch	32	
19. The Holly and the Ivy	33	
20. The First Noel	34	
21. First Noel Harmony	35	
22. We Wish You a Merry	36	
23. We Wish You Harmony	37	

www.UpadoUnlimited.com

Lyrics to Songs:

Songs 1 - 5	38
Songs 6 - 9	39
Songs 13 - 16	40
Songs 17 - 19	41
Songs 20 - 22	42
Recorder Fingering	43
Piano Fingering Chart	45

Audio Recordings are available on the website.

Greetings!

This book was created for you so that you can experience the life-changing joy that comes with making music, and so that new musicians of all ages, even those without the ability to read music, can have success playing an instrument.

All of these songs can be played with just eight notes in a C to C scale and will work with any tuned glockenspiel, xylophone, recorder, set of hand bells, piano and more. All of the music patterns are color-coded and letter-coded. Fingering charts for both piano and recorder are included to make matching the music patterns even easier.

For new musicians looking for additional songs to play, the music pattern song book *Popular 8 Note Songs* has rounds, duets, children's songs and classical pieces so that everyone can continue their learning journey.

If you have any questions or comments, please let us know. We would be happy to help you with your learning adventure at info@UpadoUnlimited.com.

MUSIC EXTRA: There are free audio tracks of many songs on our website including the songs in this music pattern song book at www.UpadoUnlimited.com.

Many Instruments to Play

The patterns of songs are the same regardless of the instrument you play. It is often easiest to start with an eight note, precision tuned glockenspiel or xylophone because these percussion instruments are simple to play. Many of them are color-coded in the same way as the patterns in this book, but if the coloring is different, you can still play along by reading the lettered notes. This will be true for hand bells as well.

A piano is also a percussion instrument, but because it does not have letters or colors on the keys, a color-coded fingering chart has been included in this book. The chart can be cut out and slipped between the piano backboard and the keys to help students find the notes of the songs.

A fingering chart for the soprano recorder has also been included. Many schools start their students with a recorder, and new musicians can actually see a visual representation of the recorder fingering placement with these music patterns. The lower the colored blocks are in the music pattern, the more fingers the student uses to cover the recorder holes.

Clarinets, flutes and pennywhistles have similar fingering patterns to the recorder, and the music patterns can be used with these instruments too.

Beginnings: Beat, Rhythm and Tone

Starting a new activity, no matter what your age is, takes courage, resources and support. In this book, music patterns for your instrument are provided to make it a little easier to take that first musical step. We encourage you to surround yourself with those who will help you learn, cheer your successes and perhaps even play along with you. Join in with your family, school class, or community group and make music together!

Beat:

The basis of all music is the beat, that steady thumping everyone is familiar within their own heartbeats. Beats are fragments of time that are all the same length. The beat can be fast or slow or somewhere in between. New musicians often need assistance maintaining a steady musical beat at first, and it can help to play along with a metronome. There are several free options online.

Rhythm:

After one learns to keep a steady beat, he or she can begin to experiment with rhythm. Rhythm is variable, and it determines the length of the notes. Music is divided into sections or measures, and many songs have four beats in every measure. In this book, the length of time to hold a beat can be determined by looking at the length of the color block. The longer the block, the more beats the note is held.

Tone:

Pitch or tone tells how low or high the note sounds to the ear. The lower notes will appear closer to the bottom of the music patterns, and the higher notes will be closer to the top. This book was created for the notes C D E F G A B C, with the lower C on the bottom of the music pattern and the higher C at the top of the music pattern.

On the next page, the length of the rhythm boxes are shown with the number of beats that each type of box receives.

Music Notes and Rhythms

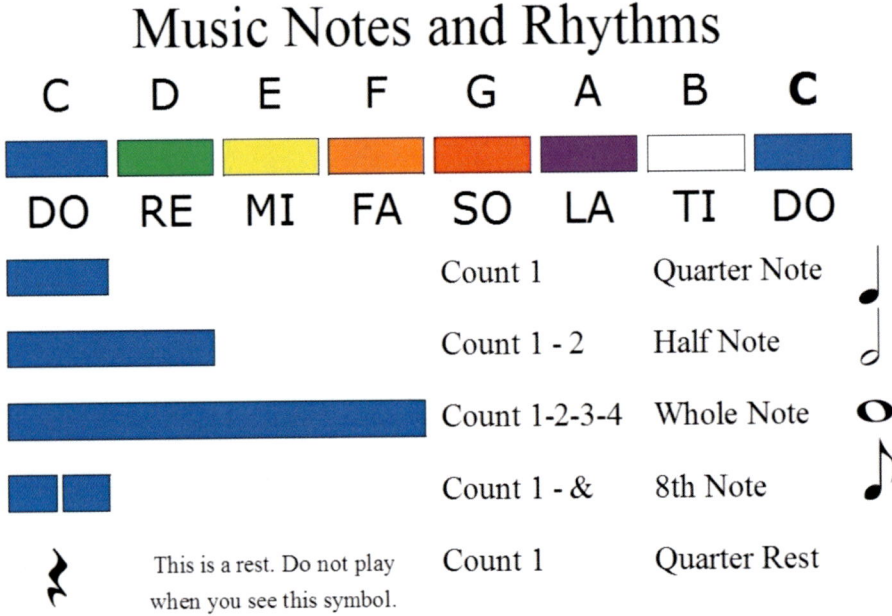

Above are the lettered notes that make up an eight note scale.
On the music patterns, a bold letter "C" will indicate the upper "C" note.

Solfege syllables are included for those who are using the Song Patterns to learn pitch and sight singing.

Artistry

Artistry:

In some of the songs in this book, artistic license was taken, and changes to either a few notes or the rhythm were made. The essence of the song is the same, and it was felt that it was better to make some changes and keep these songs approachable for new musicians rather than eliminate the songs from the collection. You are welcome to make any changes you would like as you play so that these songs are useful and enjoyable for you.

The Composer as an Artist:

In these music patterns, it is illuminating to see a visual representation of sounds that we hear. Each song has structure and repeating patterns, but each one is unique. It is interesting to contemplate what the composer of each song was thinking as he or she created these beautiful musical patterns. If you are a student of music theory, these colored patterns may give you a new perspective on the way music is put together.

Taking it Step by Step

Many parents and classroom teachers feel unequipped to teach the next generation about music because they had little opportunity to learn themselves. Sometimes, older adults who missed the chance to play an instrument when they were younger are determined to begin. Music therapists are often looking for tools to bring music to their patients. Children delight in banging the keys of a percussion instrument but need some help to know what to do next.

Yet, where does one who has not yet learned to read musical notation begin?

Most people can match colors or letters, which makes color and letter-coded music song patterns a good place to start. For those looking for instructions on how to play a glockenspiel xylophone or recorder, go to www.UpadoUnlimited.com.

The music patterns in this book start out with the most simple rhythms and then progress to more challenging pieces. The first four songs are easy tunes, and each one has four beats per measure or section. In song #5, While Shepherds Watched Their Flocks, 8th notes and rests are introduced. Now, instead of counting 1, 2, 3, 4, the count becomes 1 &, 2 &, 3 &, 4 &, giving the measure eight faster beats.

For each rest, the musician pauses for one beat or count.

Song #8, Angels We Have Heard On High, has a line that needs to be repeated before the rest of the song is played. Play Line 1 twice and then Lines 2 through 4.

The first duet is song # 9, Joy to the World. In a duet, one person plays the melody and a second person plays the harmony part. It is important that musicians go over their individual parts first before combining them with others. The teamwork skills, satisfaction and self-confidence gained are well worth the effort.

Songs #11 and #12 are Rounds. In a Round, one person begins the song, and when that person starts the second line, the next person begins to play the first line.

Starting on page 24 with song #13, there will be only three beats per measure, so the count is 1, 2, 3. A few of the songs in this section have 8th notes, so when an 8th note is present, the count becomes 1 &, 2 &, 3 &.

These music patterns are very helpful for visual learners. For those who learn best by listening, playing along with an audio recording can help. You can listen to Glockenspiel Xylophone recordings of these songs at www.UpadoUnlimited.com.

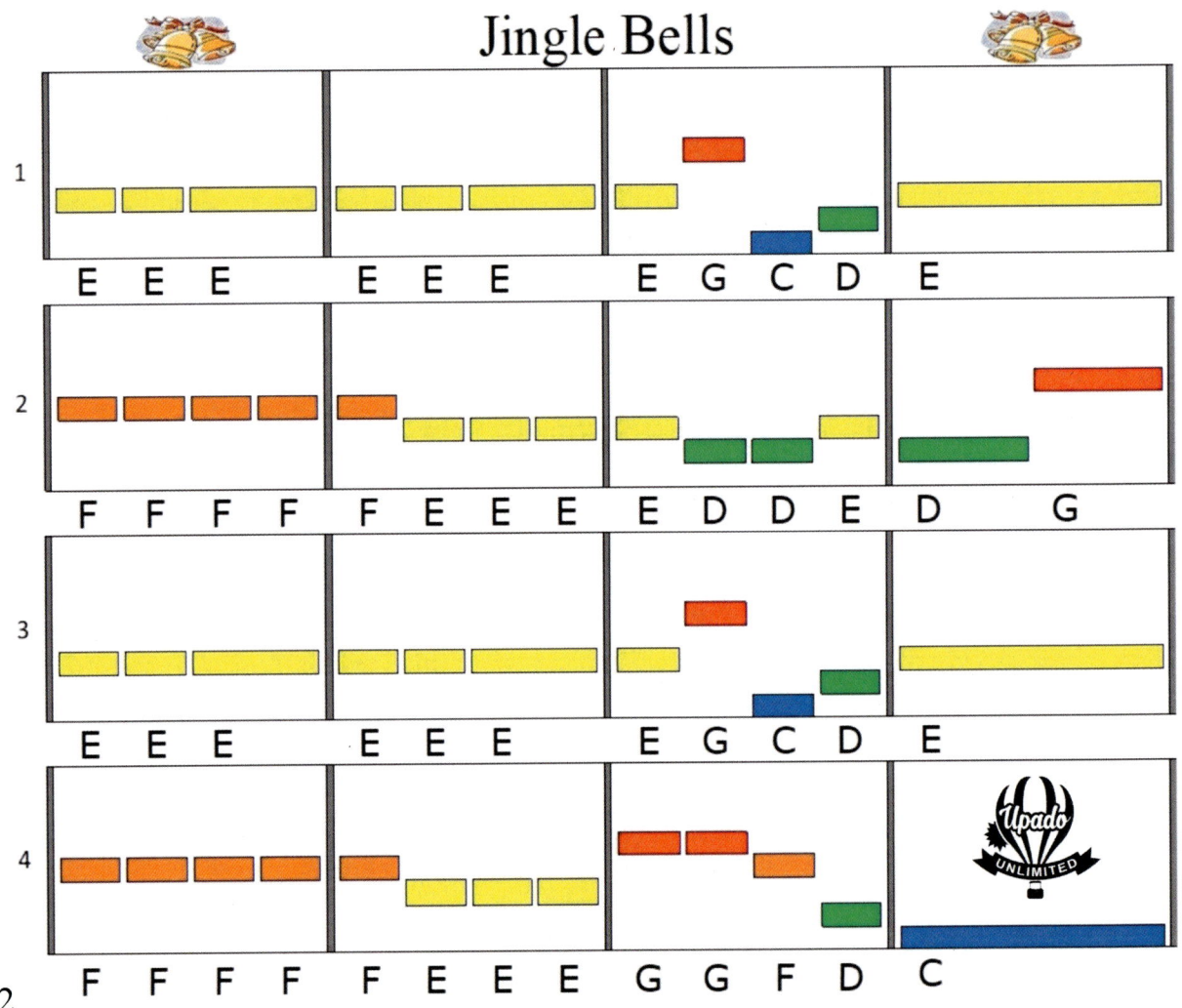

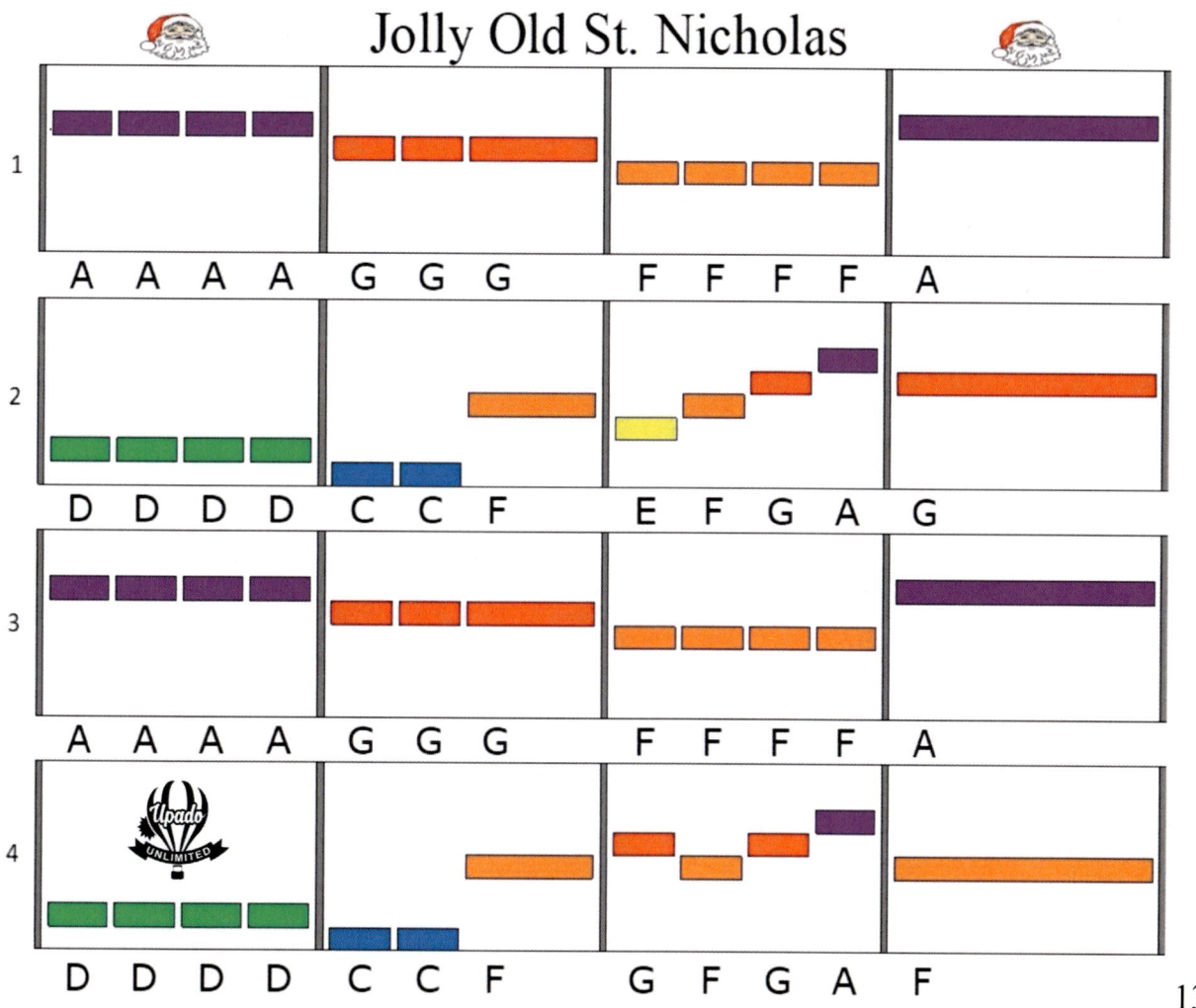

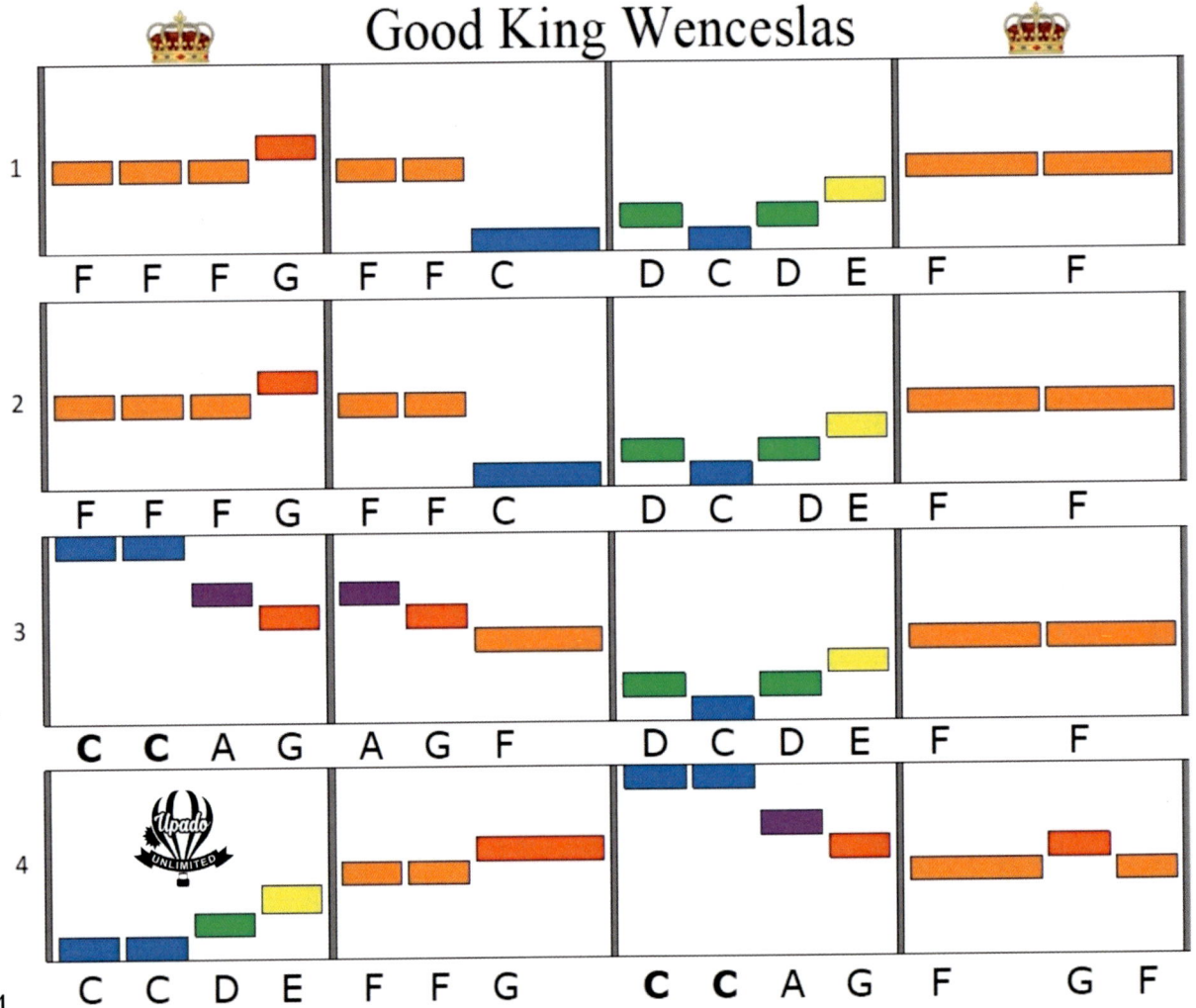

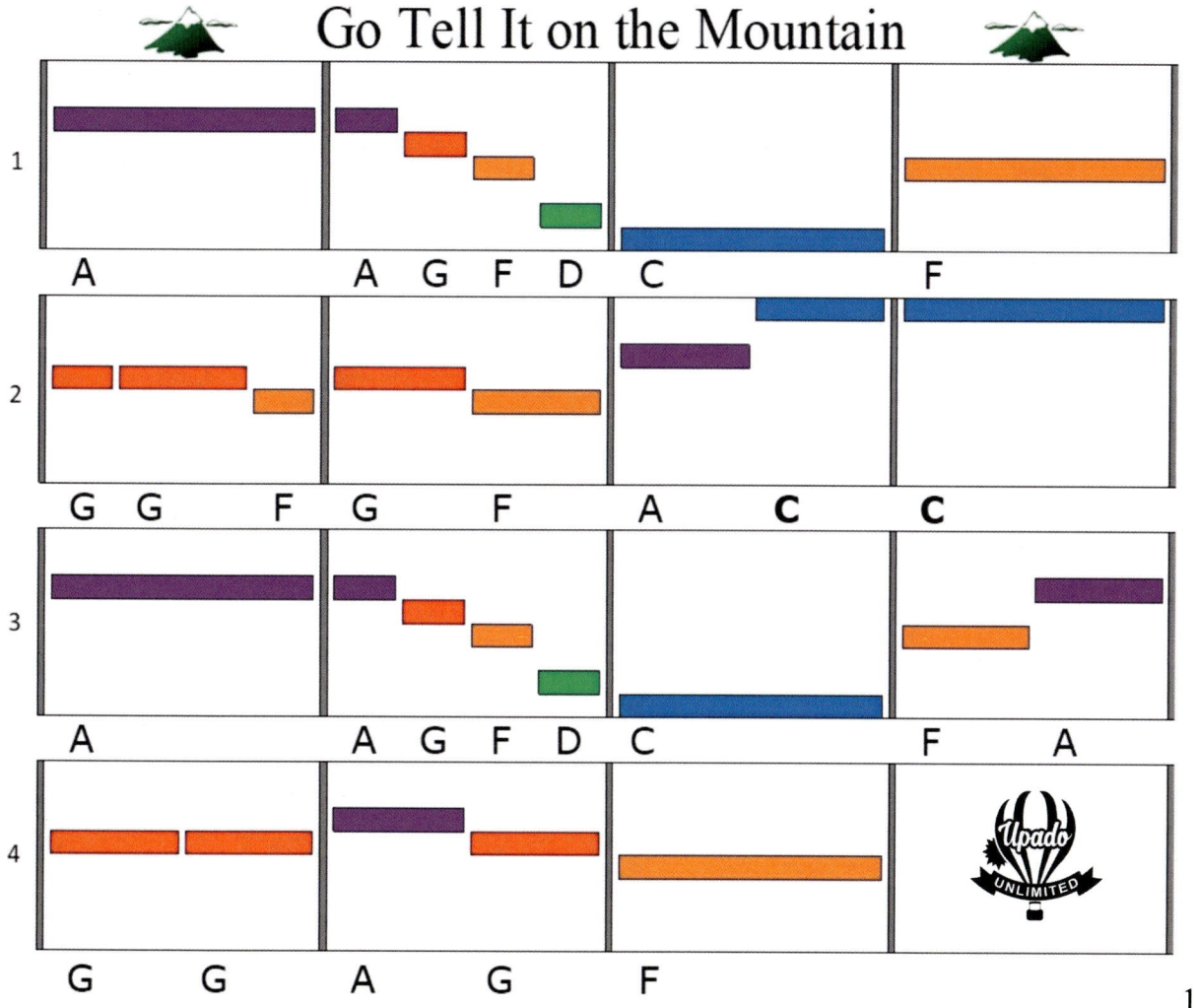

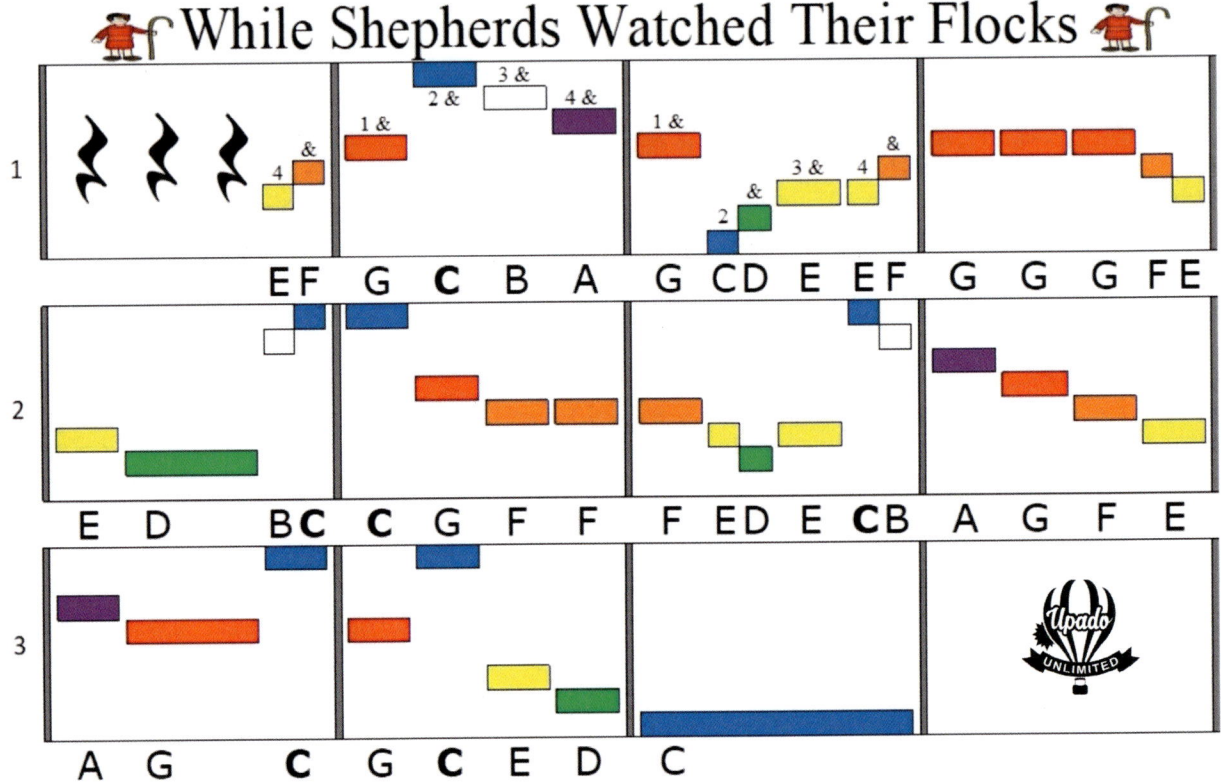

This song has three rests in the first measure. You do not play when you see a rest, just count 1 for each. It also has eighth notes. Now, instead of counting 1, 2, 3, 4 for each section or measure, you count 1& 2& 3& 4&. Quarter note color blocks that received one count before now get two. The next three songs also have 8th notes.

Up on the Housetop

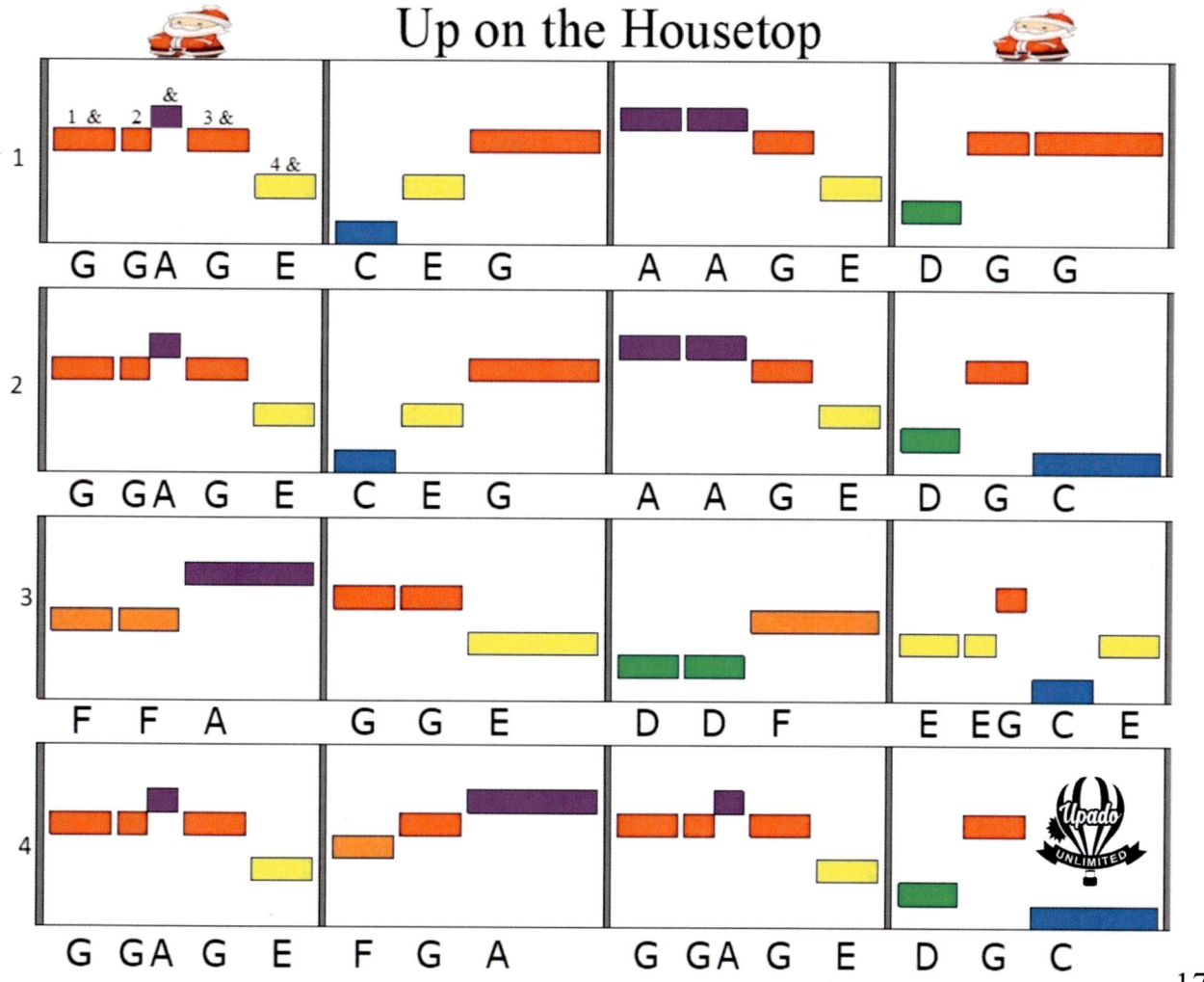

Deck the Halls

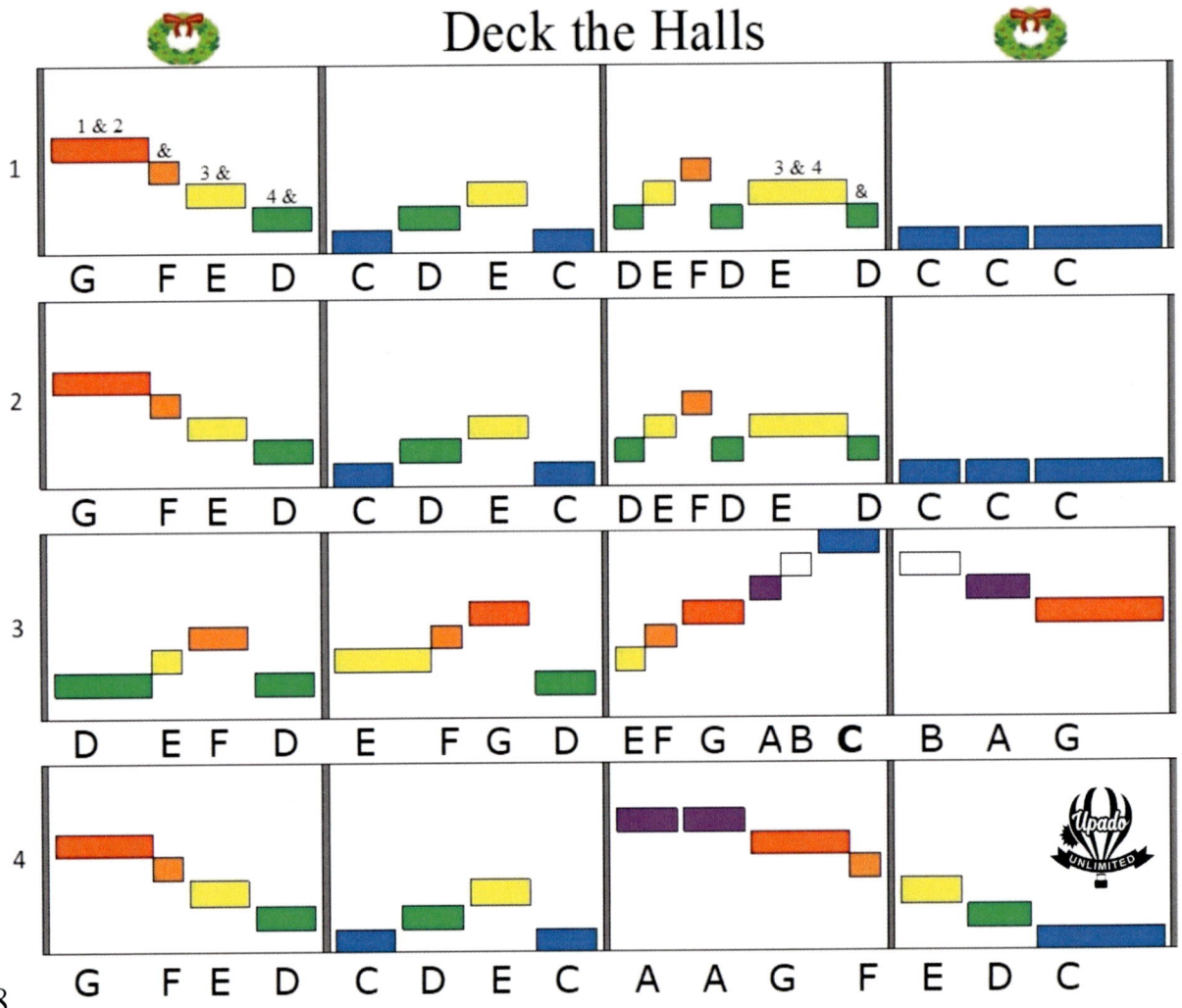

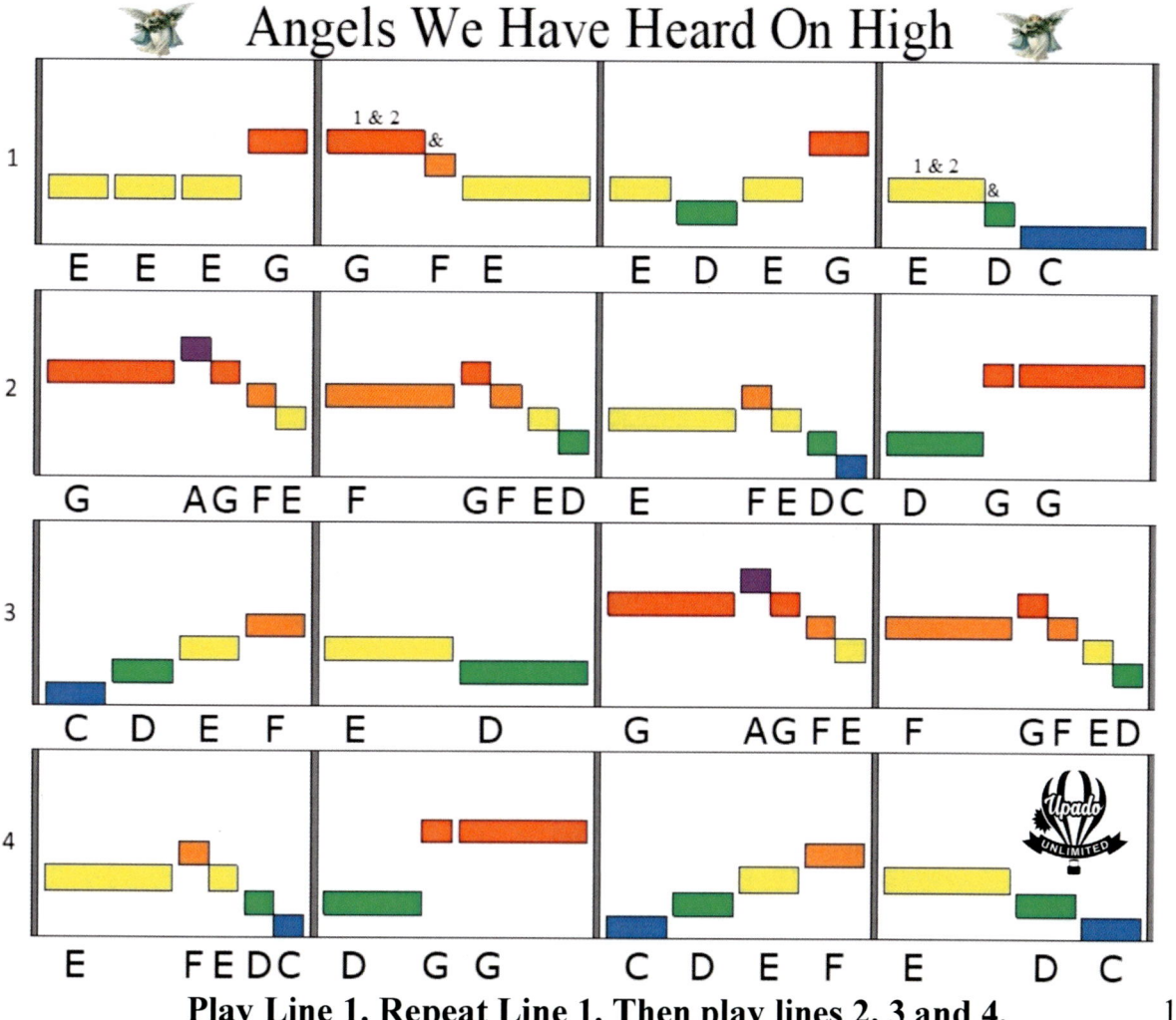

Play Line 1. Repeat Line 1. Then play lines 2, 3 and 4.

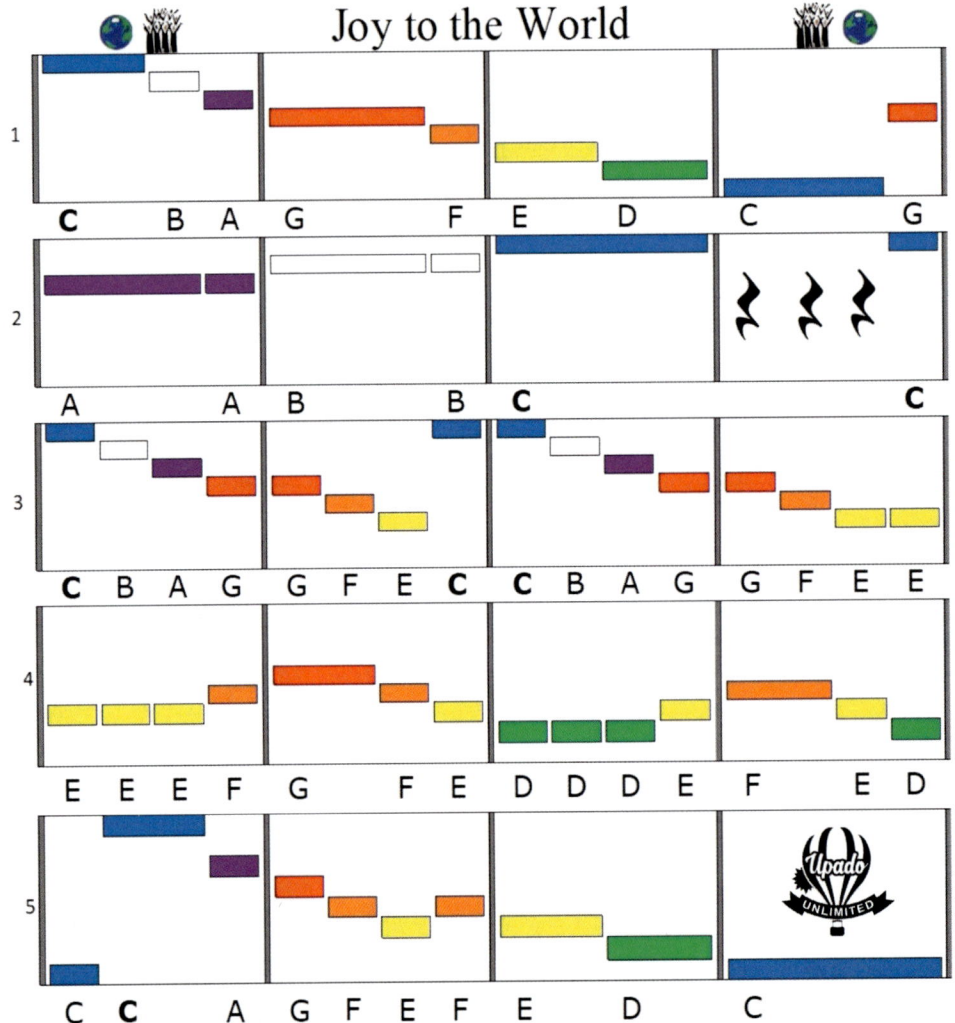

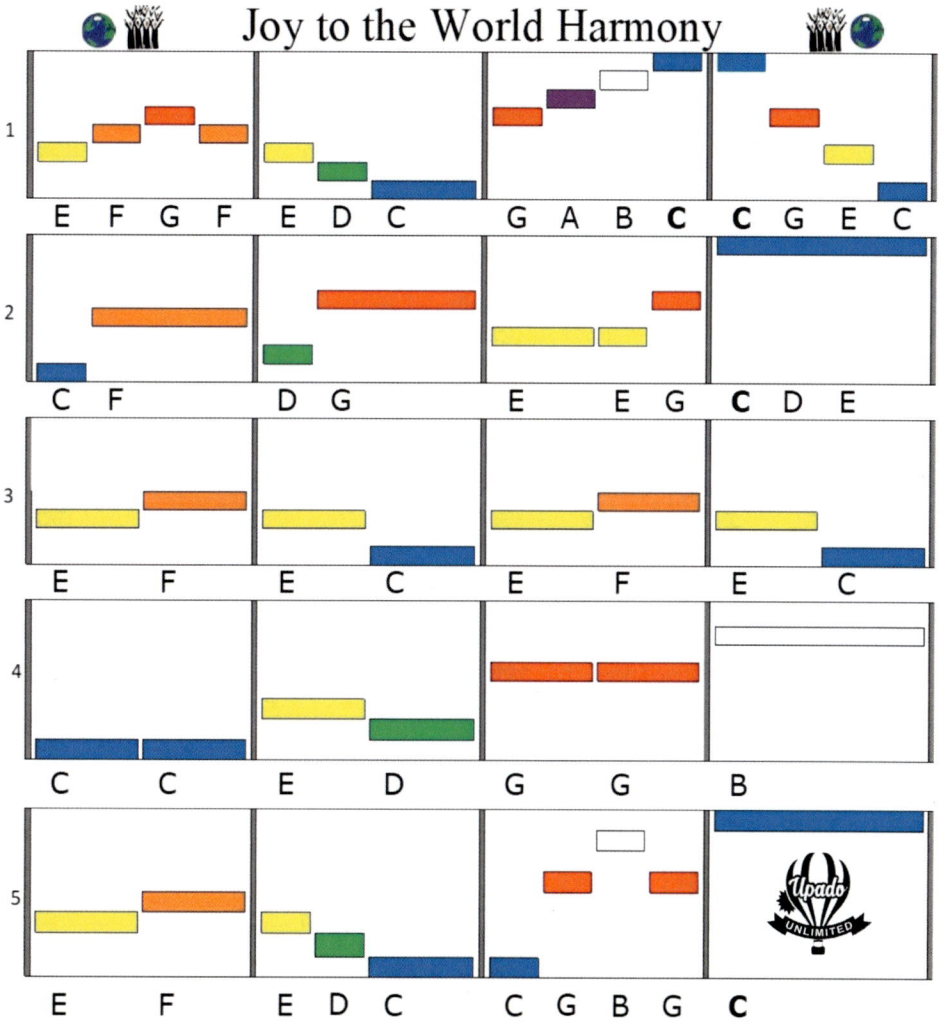

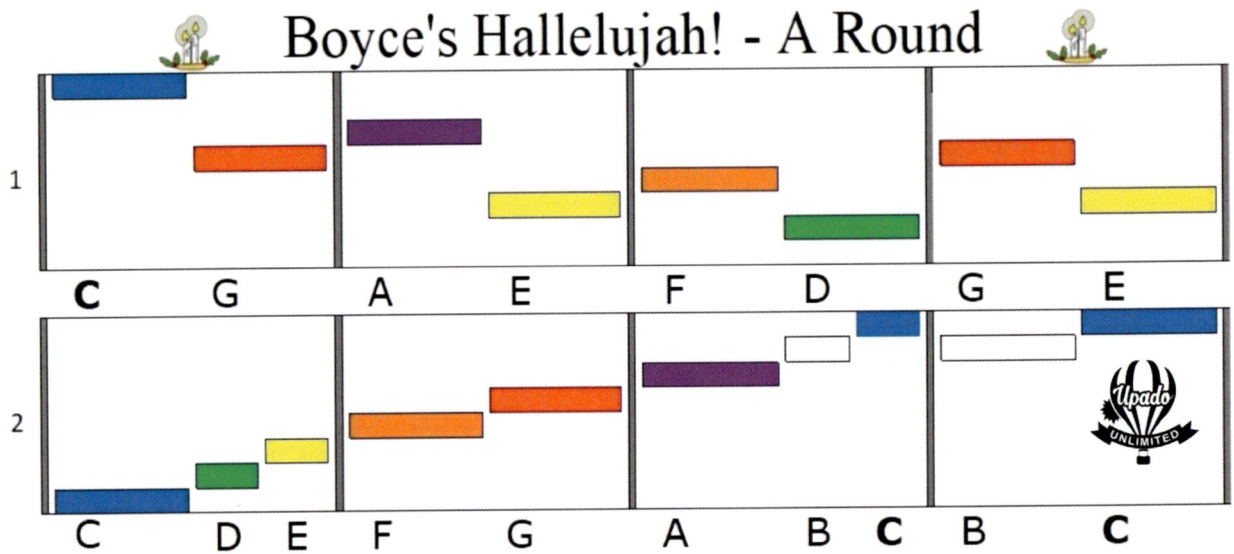

Boyce's Hallelujah and the next song, Mozart's Alleluia, are both Rounds. In a Round, one person begins the song, and when that person starts the second line, the next person begins to play the first line. When you finish the song, go back to the beginning and keep playing so you go "round and round!"

You can use two of the same instrument to play Rounds, or you can use two different instruments like a xylophone and a recorder or a piano and bells!

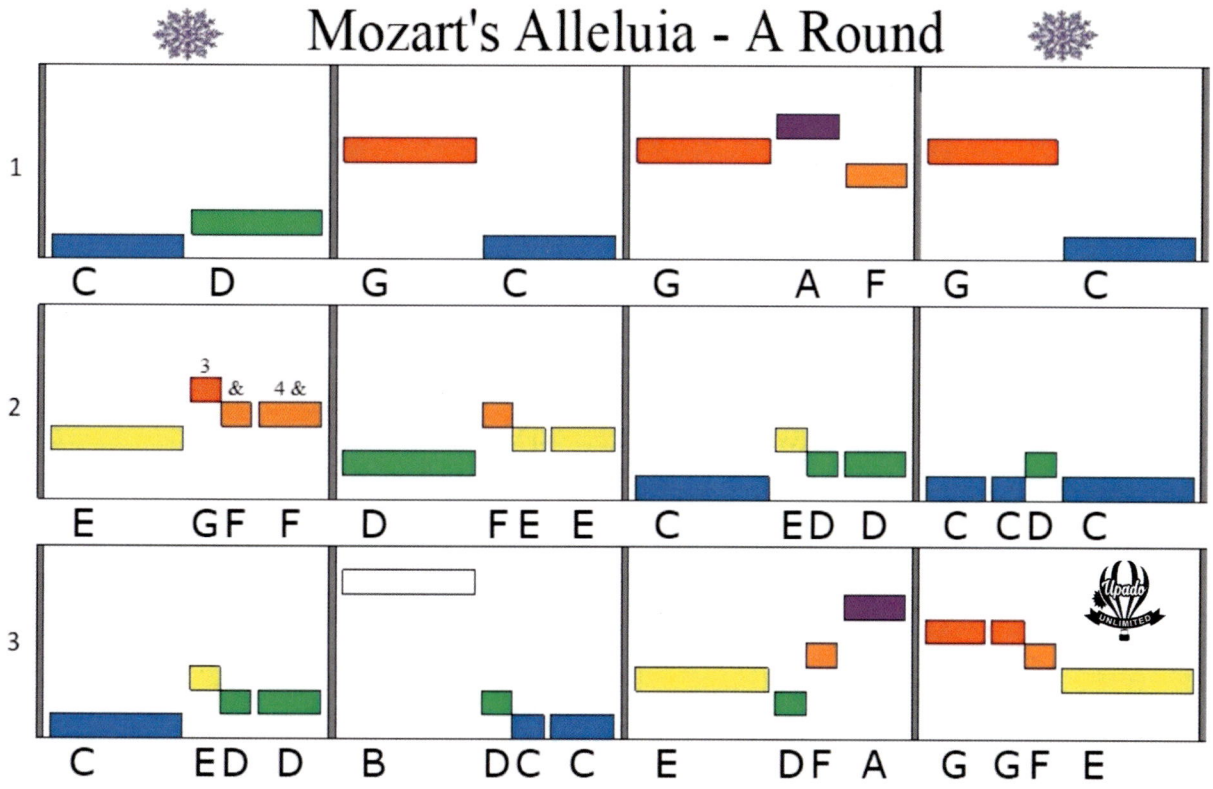

This is a Round. One person begins the song, and when that person starts the second line, the next person begins to play the first line. When the first person starts to play line three, a third person can begin the first line. Three people can play!

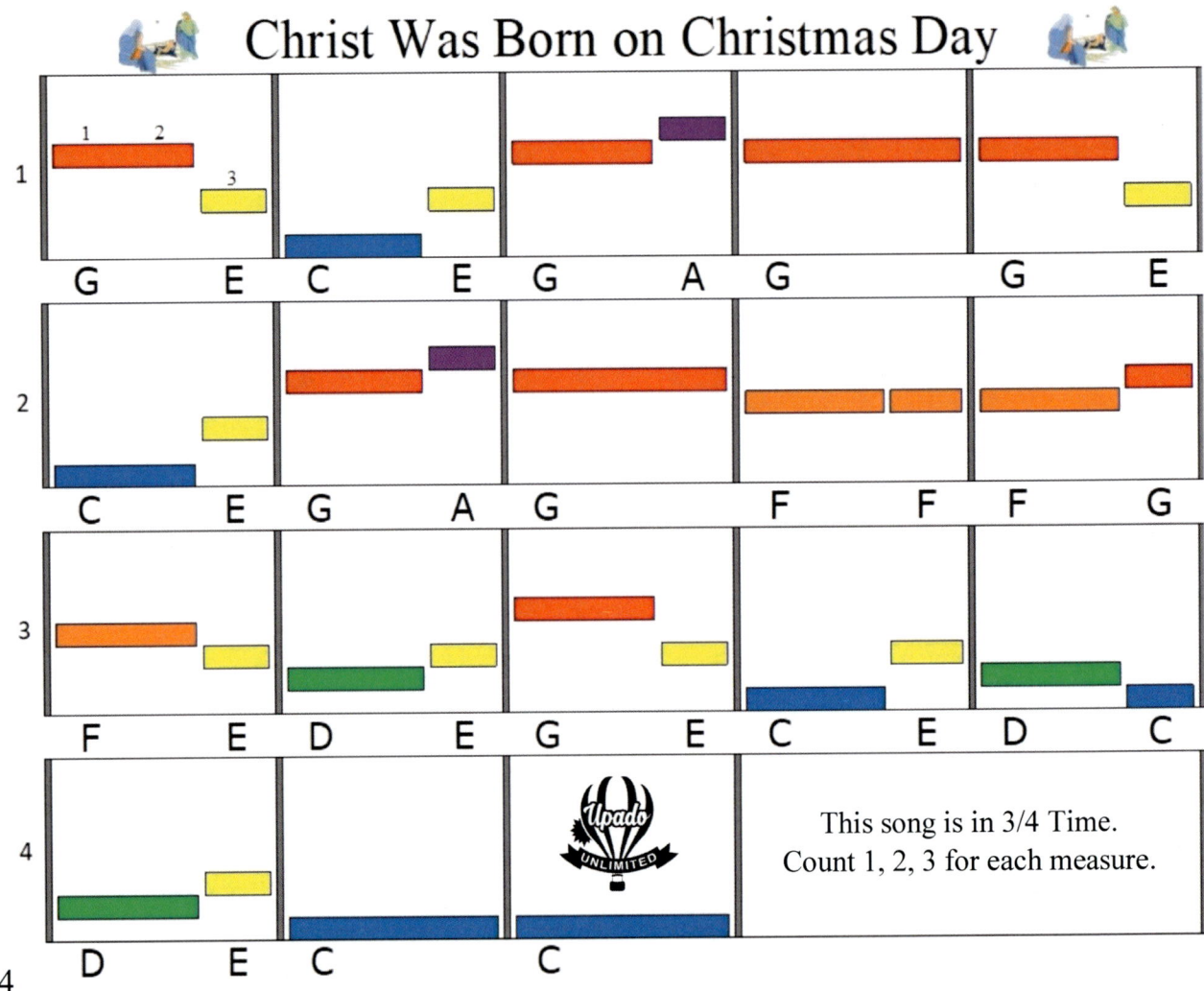

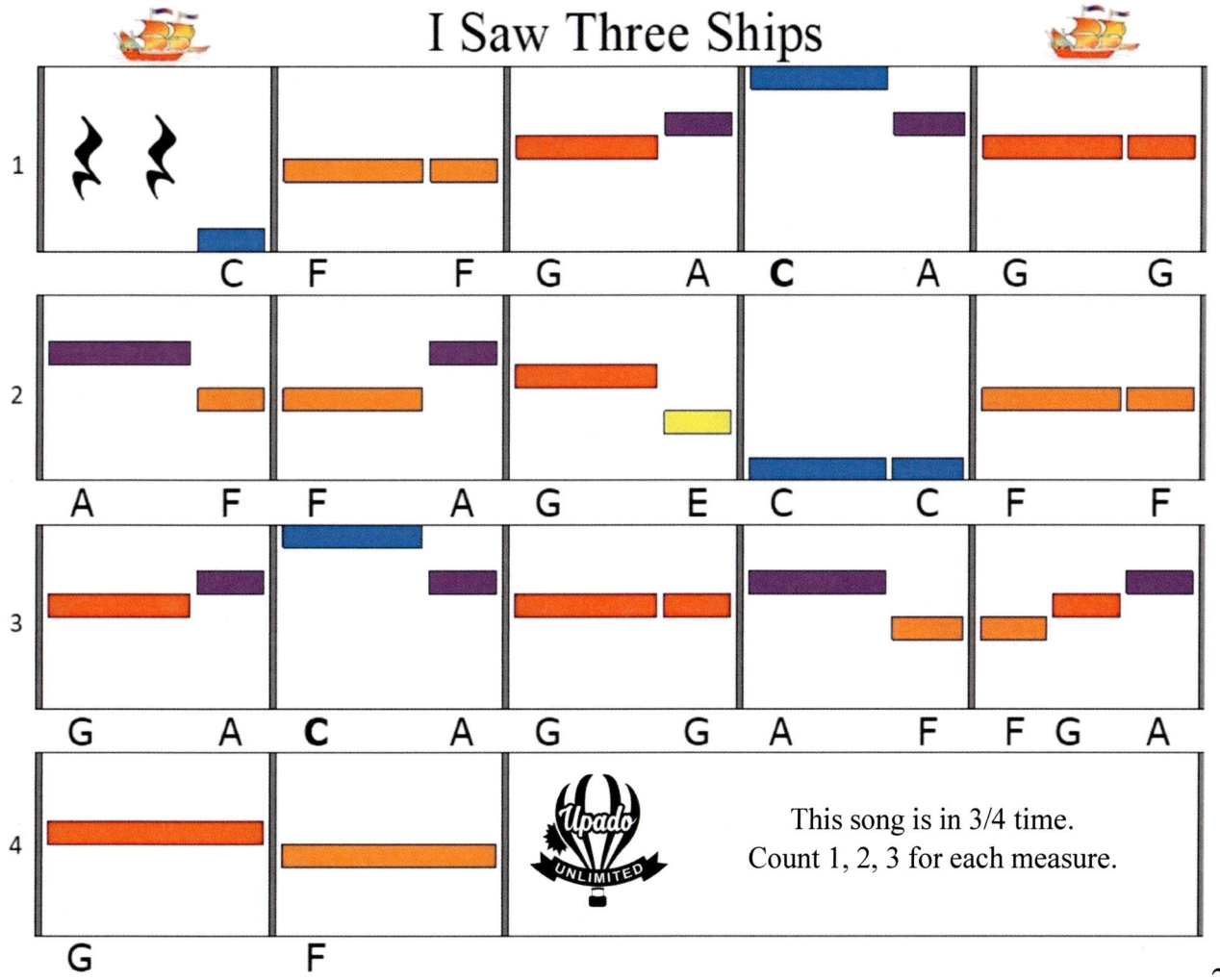

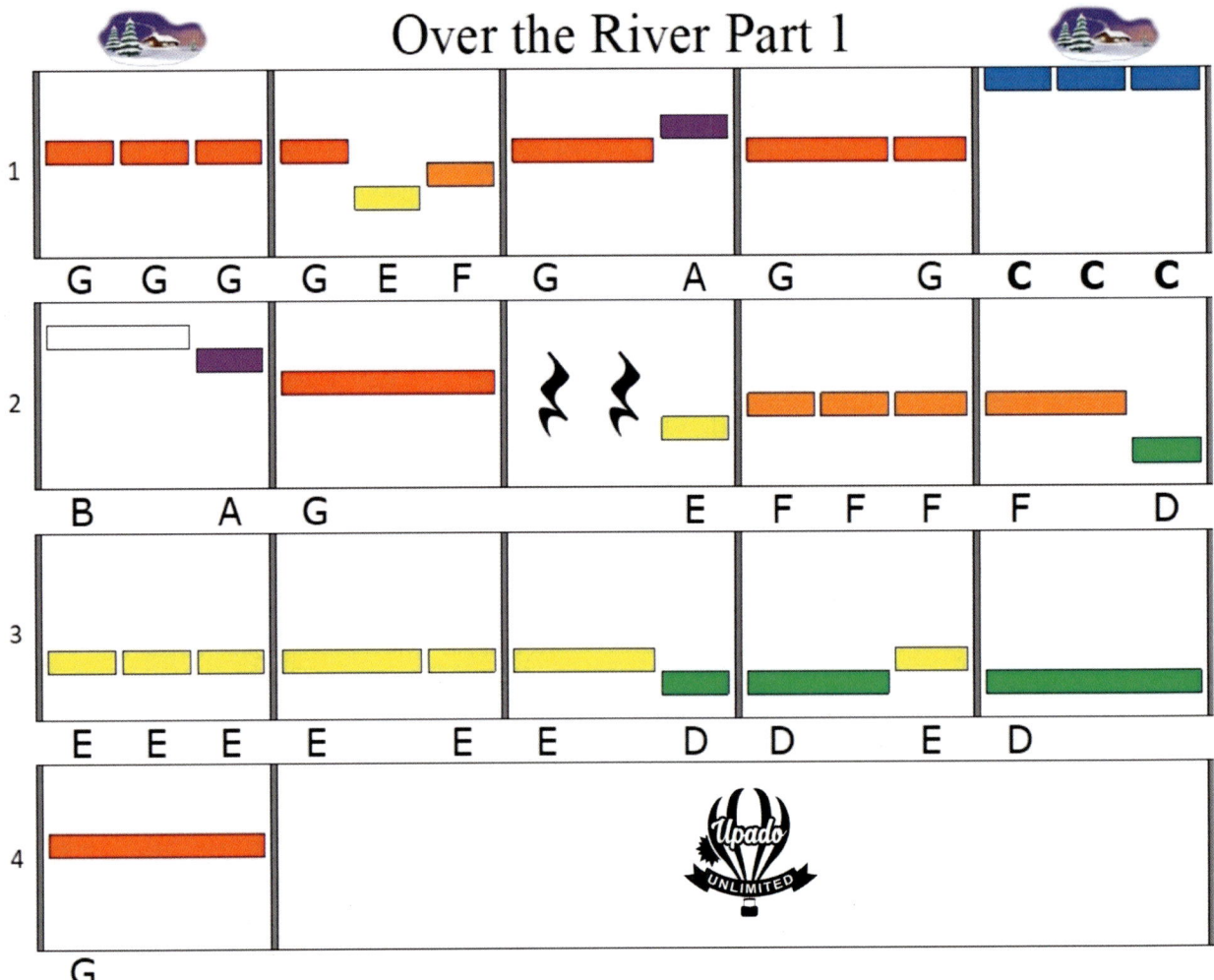

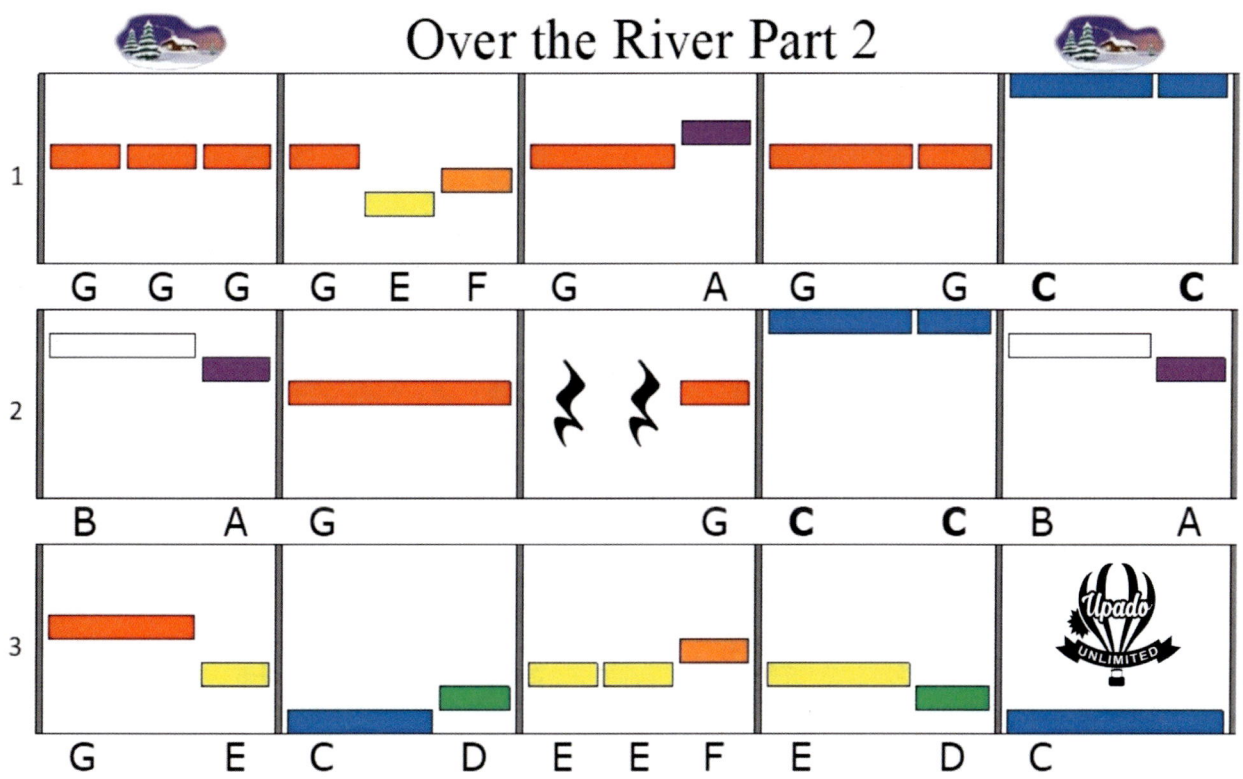

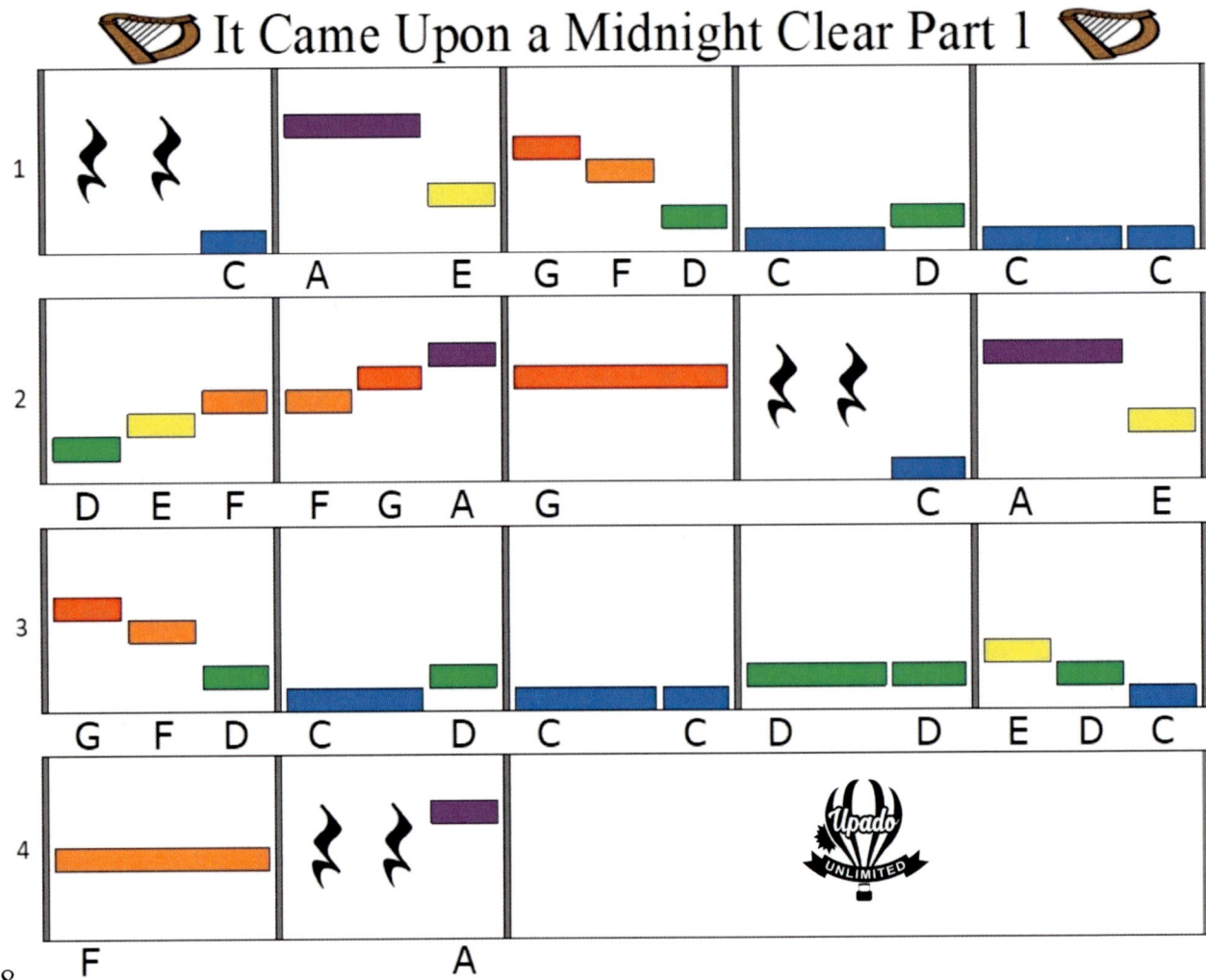

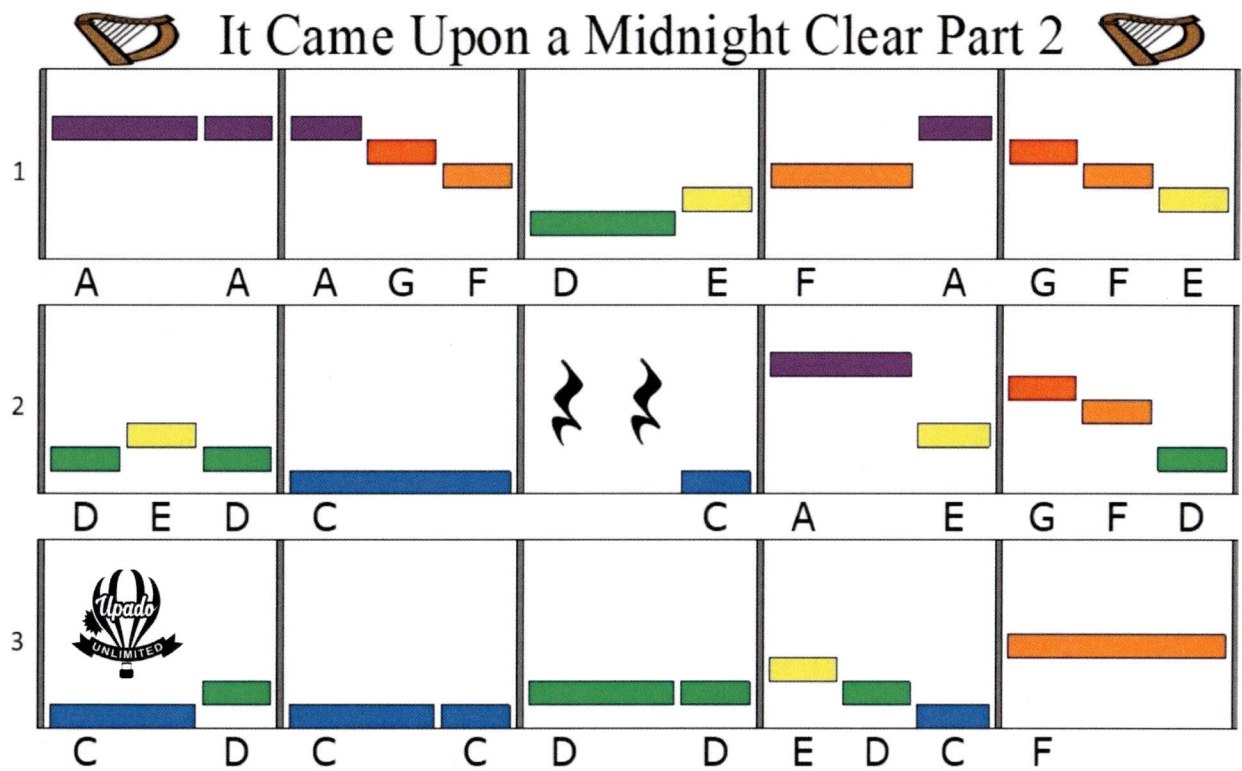

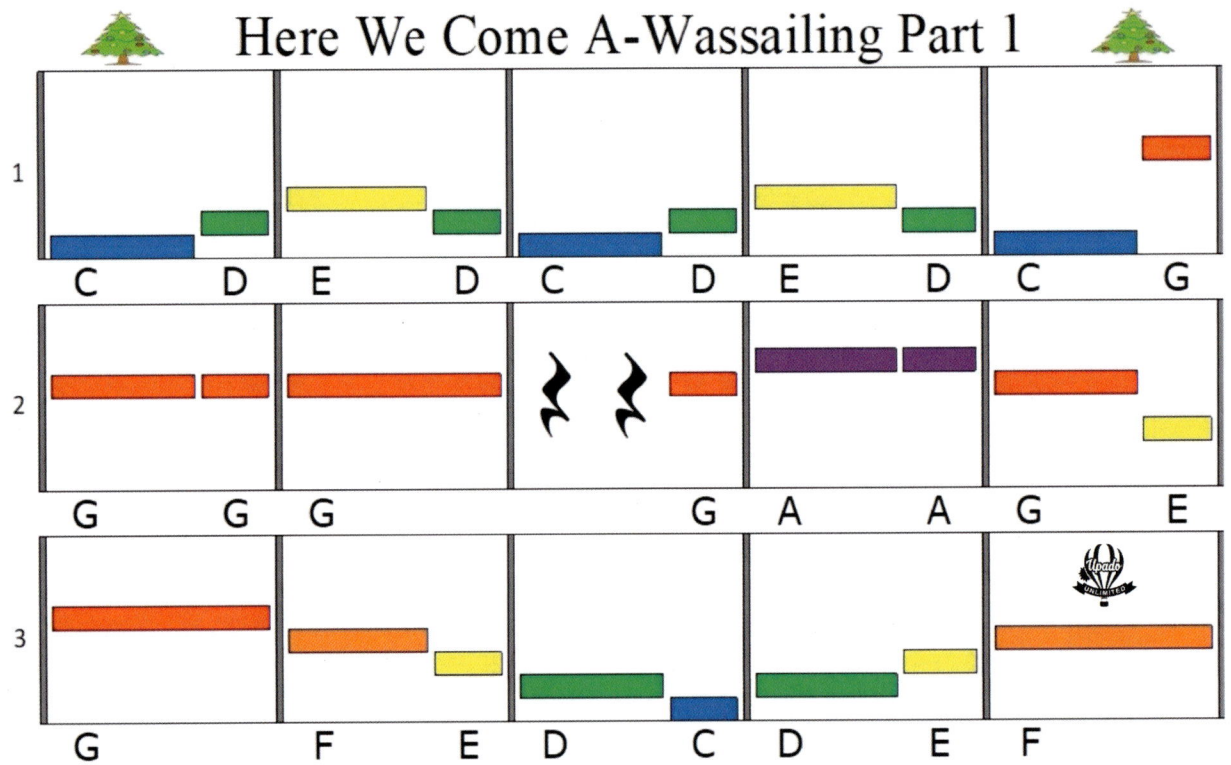

Here We Come A-Wassailing is a two part song.

The first part is in 3/4 time, so count 1, 2, 3 for each measure.

The second half of the song is in 4/4 time. Count 1, 2, 3, 4 for each measure.

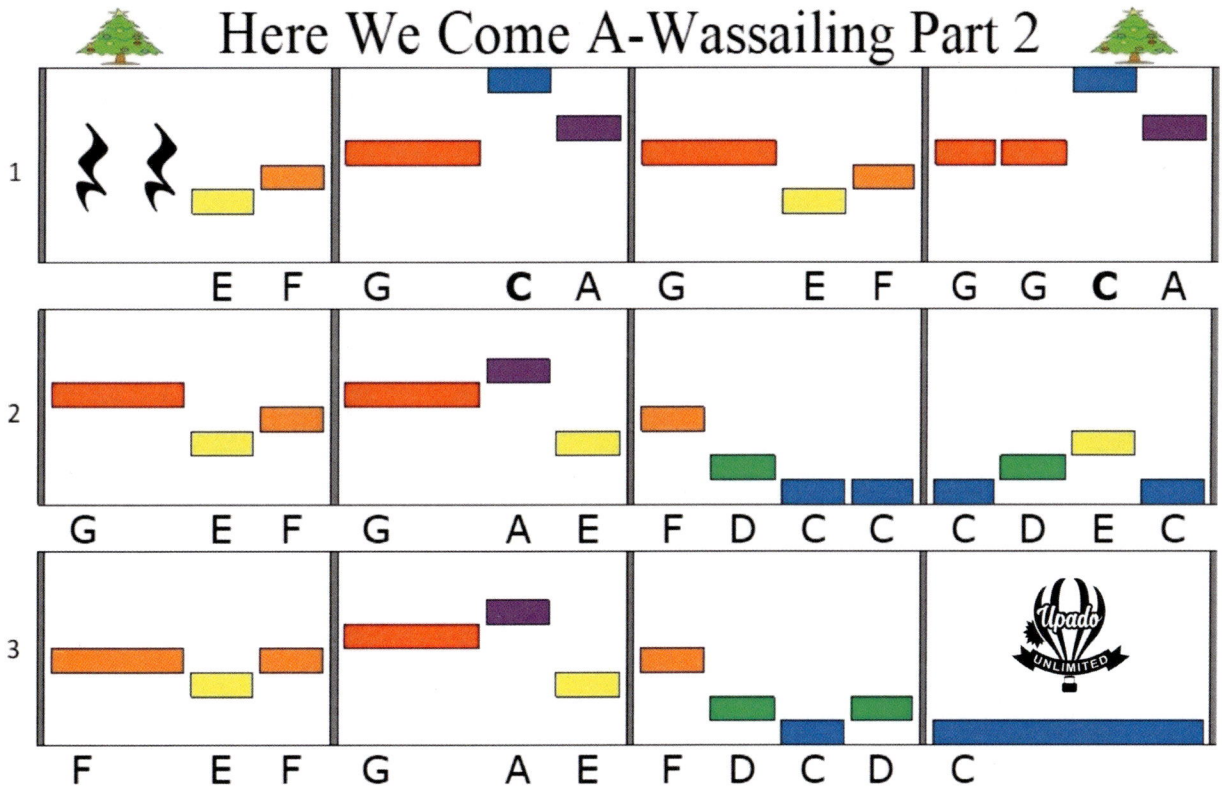

This part of Here We Come A-Wassailing is in 4/4 Time. Count 1, 2, 3, 4.

(The rest of the songs in this book will be in 3/4 time.)

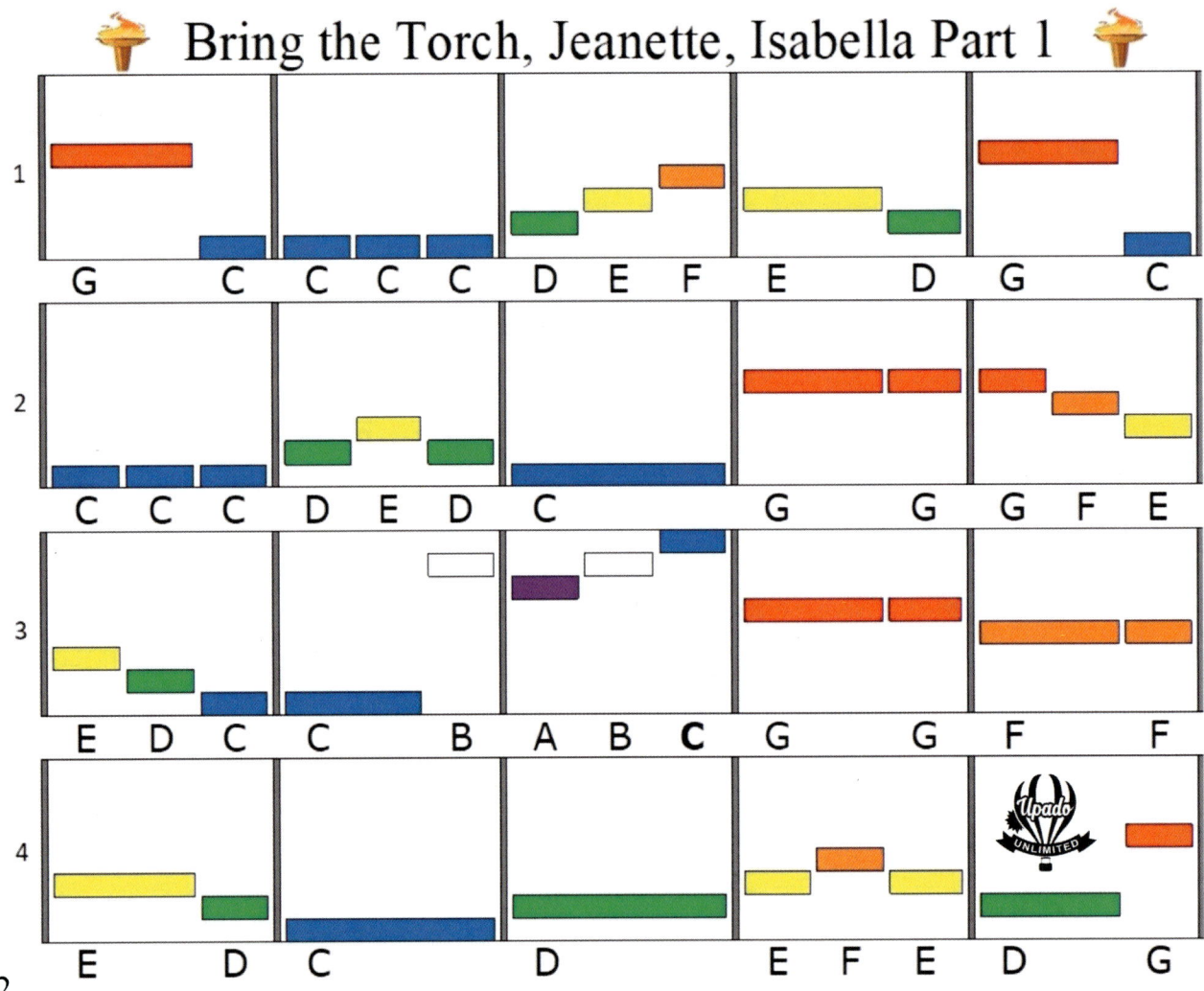

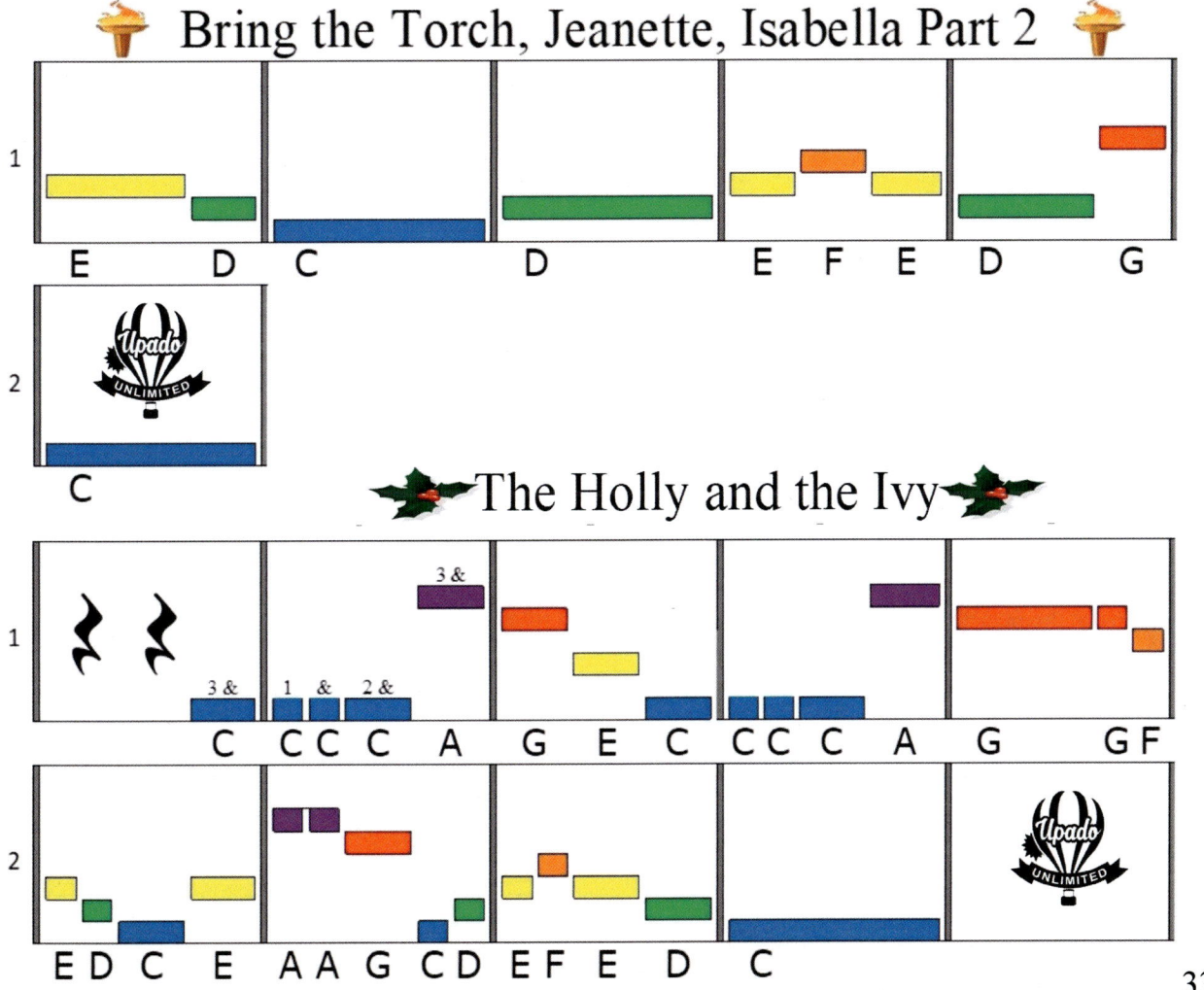

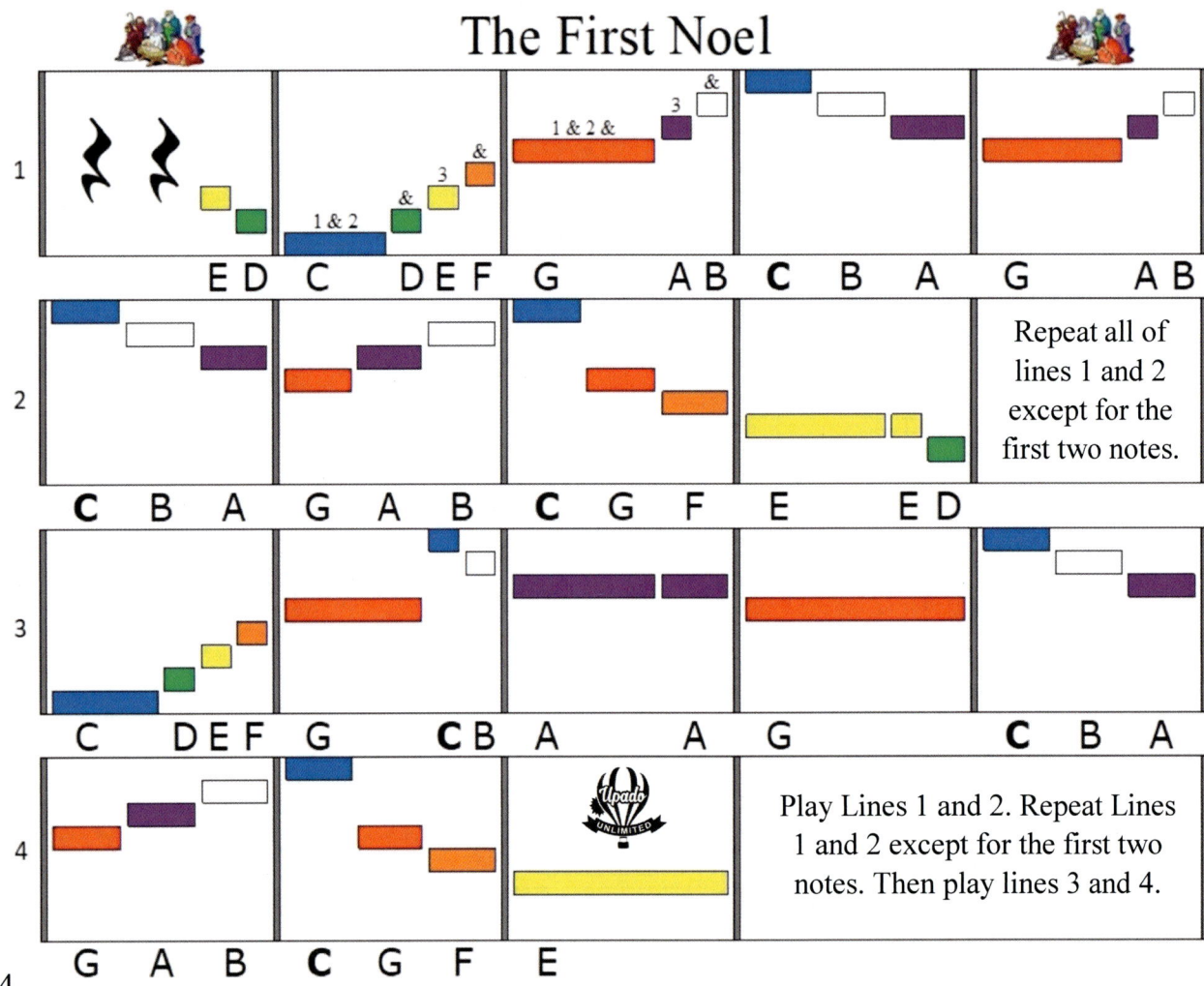

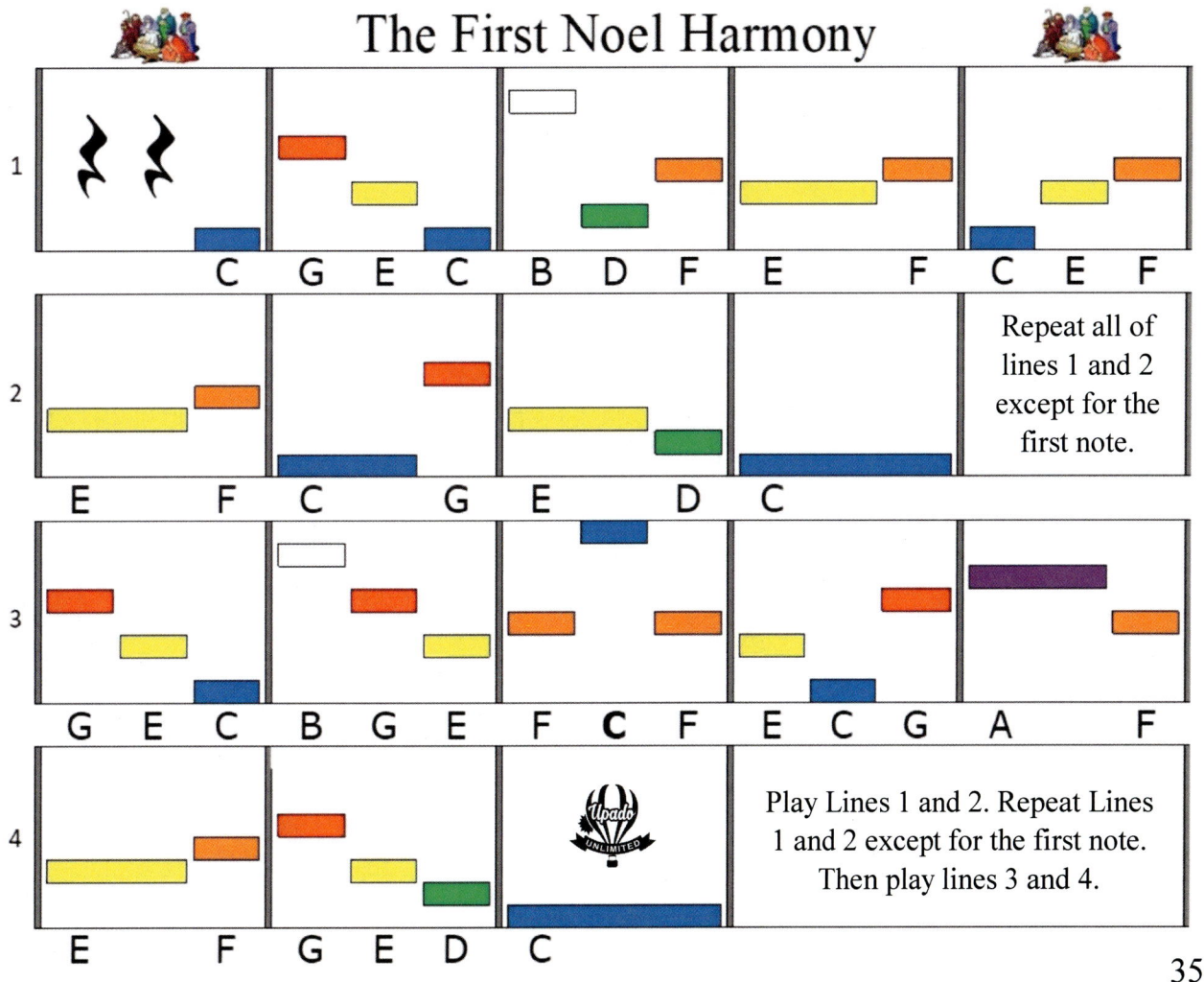

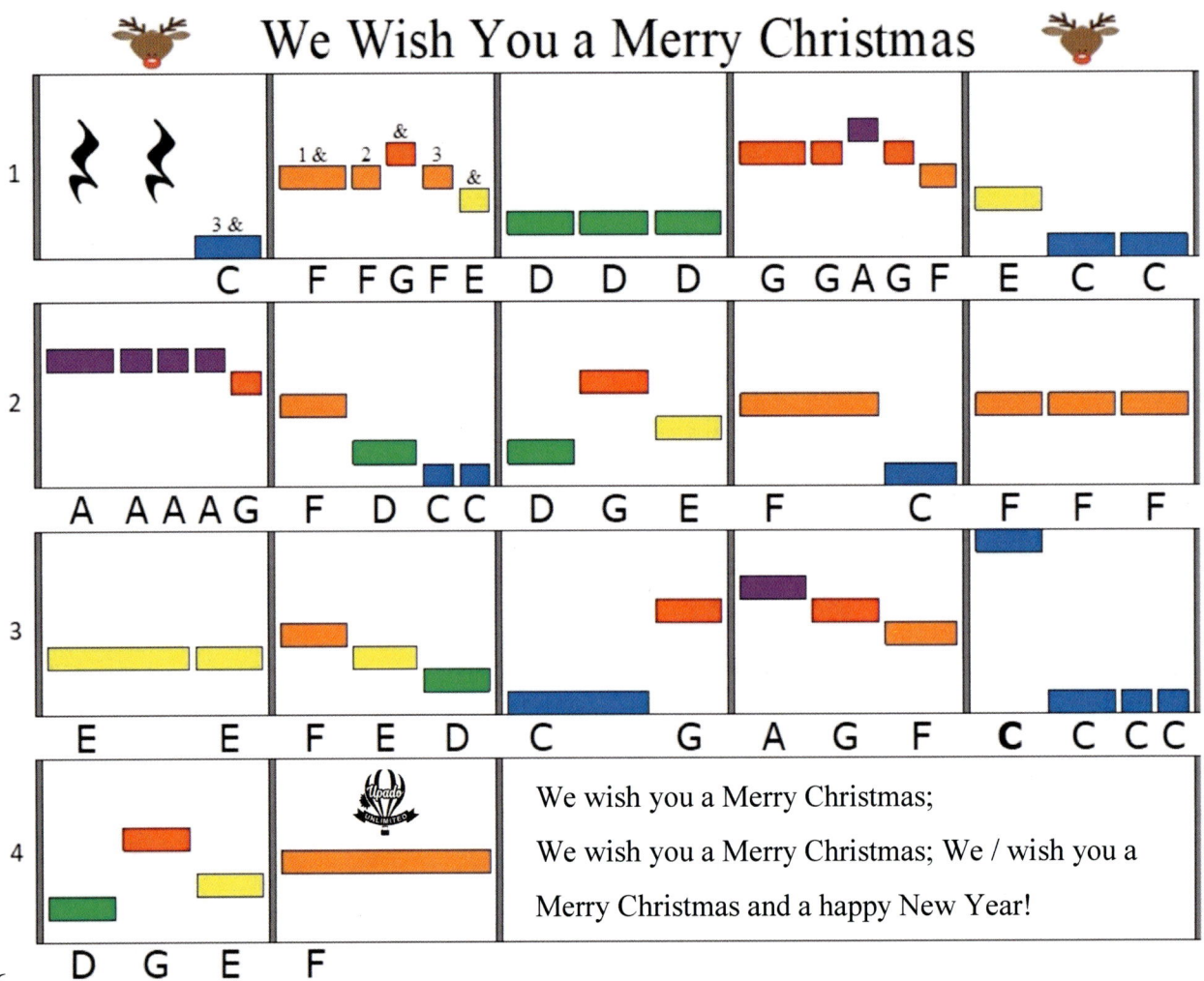

We Wish You a Merry Christmas Harmony

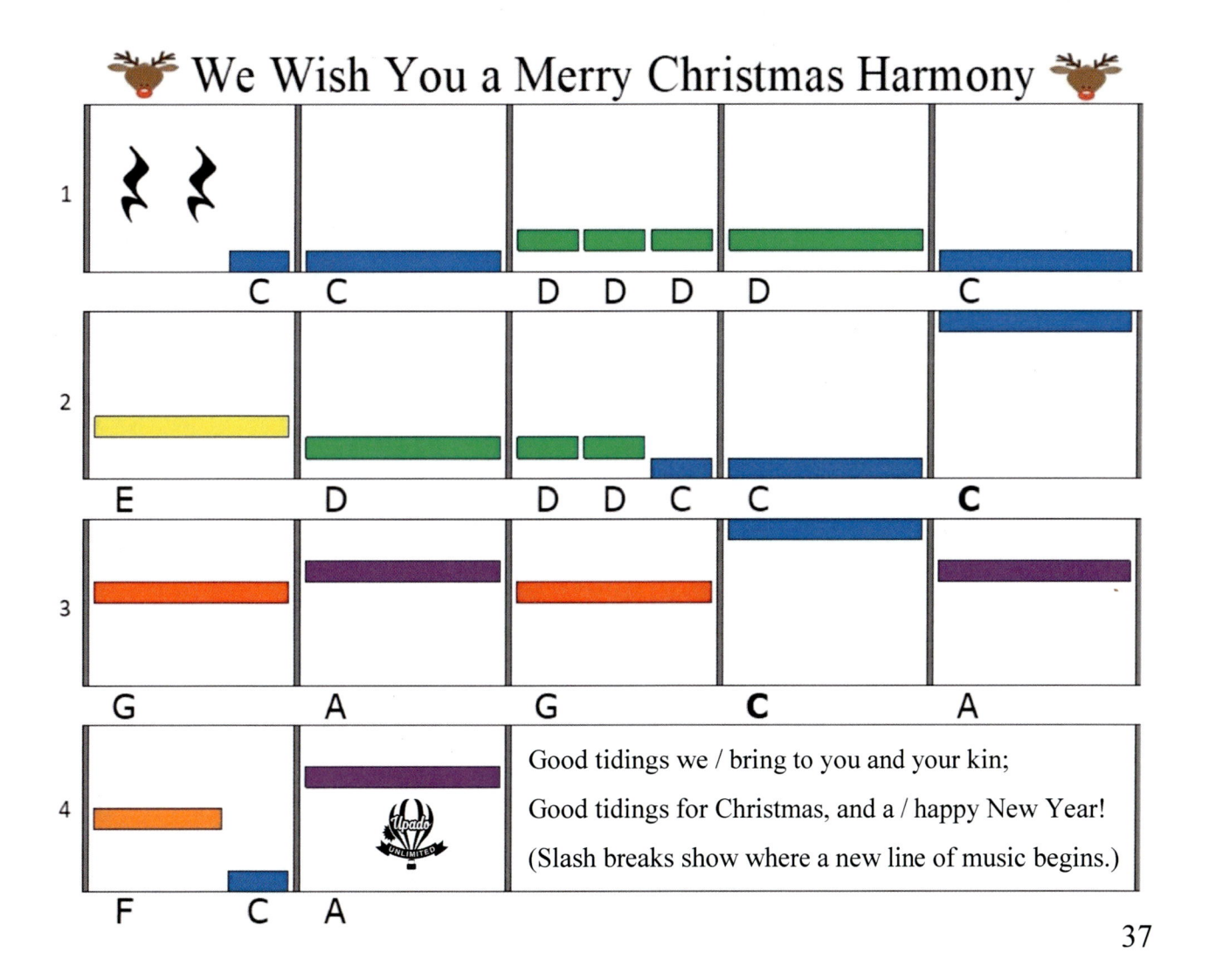

1	𝄽 𝄽	C	C	D D D	D	C

2	E	D	D D C	C	C

3	G	A	G	C	A

| 4 | F | C | A | | |

Good tidings we / bring to you and your kin;

Good tidings for Christmas, and a / happy New Year!

(Slash breaks show where a new line of music begins.)

37

Song Lyrics: *The slash break in the words indicates a new line of music on the song patterns.*

1. Jingle Bells

Jingle bells, Jingle bells, Jingle all the way / Oh, what fun it is to ride in a one-horse open sleigh /

Jingle bells, Jingle bells, Jingle all the way / Oh, what fun it is to ride in a one-horse open sleigh.

2. Jolly Old St. Nicholas

Jolly old St. Nicholas, Lean your ear this way / Don't you tell a single soul, What I'm going to say /

Christmas Eve is coming soon, Now, you dear old man / Whisper what you'll bring to me: Tell me if you can.

3. Good King Wenceslas

Good King Wenceslas looked out on the Feast of Stephen / When the snow lay 'round about deep

and crisp and even / Brightly shone the moon that night though the frost was cruel/

When a poor man came in sight gath'ring winter fuel.

4. Go Tell It on the Mountain

Go, tell it on the mountain / over the hills and everywhere / Go, tell it on the mountain / that Jesus Christ is born

5. While Shepherds Watched Their Flocks

While shepherds watched their flocks by night, all seated on the / ground,

An angel of the Lord came down, and glory shone / around, and glory shone around.

6. Up on the Housetop

Up on the housetop reindeer pause, out jumps good ol' Santa Claus /

Down through the chimney with lots of toys, all for the little ones, Christmas joy /

Ho ho ho, who wouldn't go, Ho ho ho, who wouldn't go-o/

Up on the housetop, click, click, click. Down through the chimney with good Saint Nick.

7. Deck the Halls

Deck the halls with boughs of holly, Fa la la la la la la la! / 'Tis the season to be jolly, Fa la la la la la la la! /

Don we now our gay apparel, Fa la la la la la la la! / Troll the ancient Yuletide carol, Fa la la la la la la la!

8. Angels We Have Heard on High

Angels we have heard on high, sweetly singing o'er the plains /

And the mountains in reply, echoing their joyous strains /

Gloria, / in excelsis Deo. Glo /ria, in excelsis Deo.

9. Joy to the World

Joy to the world the Lord is come Let / earth receive her king

Let / every heart prepare him room And / heaven and nature sing, and heaven and nature sing

And / heaven and heaven and nature sing.

13. Christ Was Born on Christmas Day

Christ was born on Christmas Day. Wreath the / holly, twine the bay;

Christmas natus / hodie; the Babe, the Son, the Holy / One of Mary.

14. I Saw Three Ships

I saw three ships come sailing in on / Christmas Day, on Christmas Day

I saw three / ships come sailing in on Christmas Day in the / morning.

15. Over the River and Through the Woods

Over the river and through the woods, to grandmother's / house we go;

The horse knows the way to / carry the sleigh, through the white and drifted snow! / Oh! /

Over the river and through the woods, Oh, how the / wind does blow!

It stings the toes and / bites the nose, As over the ground we go.

16. It Came Upon a Midnight Clear

It came upon the midnight clear, that / glorious song of old

From angels / bending near the earth to touch their harps of / gold

Peace / on the earth goodwill to men, from Heaven's all / gracious King

The world in solemn / stillness lay to hear the angels sing.

17. Here We Come A-Wassailing

Here we come a-wassailing among the / leaves so green, Here we come a / wand'ring, so fair to be seen. /

Love and joy come to you, and to you glad Christmas / too,

And God bless you, and send you a Happy New / Year, and God send you a Happy New Year.

18. Bring a Torch, Jeanette, Isabella

Bring a torch, Jeanette, Isabelle! Bring a / torch, to the stable call

Christ is born, Tell the / folk of the village. Jesus is born and Mary's / calling.

Ah! Ah! beautiful is the / Mother! Ah! Ah! beautiful is her / child.

19. The Holly and the Ivy

The holly and the ivy, when they are both full grown

Of / all the trees that are in the wood, the holly bears the crown.

The rising of the sun, and the running of the deer,

The / playing of the merry organ, Sweet singing of the choir.

20. The First Noel

The First Noel, the Angels did say was to / certain poor shepherds in fields as they lay

In / fields where they lay keeping their sheep on a / cold winter's night that was so deep.

No / el, Noel, Noel, Noel; Born is the / King of Israel!

22. We Wish You a Merry Christmas

We wish you a Merry Christmas; We wish you a Merry Christmas;

We / wish you a Merry Christmas and a happy New Year!

Good tidings we / bring to you and your kin;

Good tidings for Christmas, and a / happy New Year!

Thank you so much for purchasing a copy of this book! I hope you have a wonderful time making musical memories with your family, friends or classmates this Christmas season. If you have any questions or comments, I would be happy to help you at info@UpadoUnlimited.com.

Wishing you all the best, Debra

Recorder Fingering Chart

You can remove this page to use as a reference, or if you would prefer to keep this page intact, you can email us at info@UpadoUnlimited.com, and we will send you a free PDF file of this page for you to use instead of removing this one from your book.

		C	D	E	F	G	A	B	C
Left Hand	Thumb	●	●	●	●	●	●	○	●
	1	●	●	●	●	●	●	○	●
	2	●	●	●	●	●	●	●	●
	3	●	●	●	●	●	●	●	●
Right Hand	4	●	●	●	●	●	●	●	●
	5	●	●	●	●	●	●	●	●
	6	●●	●●	●●	●●	●●	●●	●●	●●
	7	●●	●●	●●	●●	●●	●●	●●	●●

Extra Info:

With some recorders, the "F" note is played by covering all of the holes except for the #5 hole.

Piano Keyboard Fingering Chart

You can remove this page and cut out the Piano Keyboard Rectangle with the letters and colors below. Place the chart between the back of the keys and the backboard of the piano so you can match the colors and letters of the keys to the music patterns in this song book!

C	D	E	F	G	A	B	C

If you would prefer to keep this page intact, you can email us at info@UpadoUnlimited.com, and we will send you a free PDF file of this page for you to use instead of removing this one from your book.

Made in the USA
Las Vegas, NV
10 November 2024